Foundations of Founding

by Alan Clayton

Copyright

ISBN 978-1-912328-06-2

Foundations of Founding

by Alan Clayton

@thealanclayton

alannotatwork@gmail.com

Foundations
of Founding

How was your day? Get everything done? Get the important stuff done? Created a legacy worth dying for?

Me neither!! But I'm working on it, and that's what's exciting. And here's how.

My own journey has taken me from business school, via the Walmart corporation and 20+ years coaching the good, bad and ugly in the corporate world (think Unilever, Motorola, AT&T, GSK, Virgin) to founding five businesses of my own, to my last seven years mentoring over 1000 startup founders backed by the world's largest investor in early stage startups, and contributing to accelerator programs around the world.

This unassuming handbook contains the basic tools that have stood the test of time and been distilled from all I heard, read about, saw and learned by experience on the way.

At my best I buy hotels without any money, walk on fire, create Fairtrade towns, run marathons, and share time with...well... just other people with dreams, turning as many as possible into reality.

I didn't invent much; I'm just passing on what I've seen generate actual tangible results, especially for startup founders.

Enjoy!

Alan Clayton

Foundations of Founding

by Alan Clayton

Yes, they work!

"I got a lot from it, enjoyed it, and some found it quite mind-blowing."

Human Resources Manager, Body Shop

"Probably the best money Unilever could spend on an employee."

Employee Development Manager,
Unilever Research

"Thank you for helping me grow as a person when we were at HAX earlier in the year. I will be forever grateful."

D.G., founder, HAX

"I got my best advice from you which is really going to help me in boosting my startup."

G.L., founder, Chinaccelerator

Foundations of Founding

by Alan Clayton

What are they?

1 Have a Vision

If you have a big enough 'why', the 'how tos' will show up.

You can't do it!

Says who?!

▶ **Example: Henry Ford**
"I will build a car for the great multitude. It will be large enough for the family, but small enough for the individual to run and care for. It will be constructed of the best materials, by the best men to be hired, after the simplest designs that modern engineering can devise. But it will be so low in price that no man making a good salary will be unable to own one — and enjoy with his family the blessing of hours of pleasure in God's great open spaces."

Example: Lord Lever (Unilever)
"To make cleanliness commonplace; to lessen work for women; to foster health and contribute to personal attractiveness, that life may be more enjoyable and rewarding for the people who use our products."

▶ A vision, as the word suggests, is a vivid description or picture of a compelling end result. At its best it is sufficient to guide all staff activities when the CEO leaves the building.

1 Vision into Action

Recipe for Frustration

Henry Ford's Vision:

"I will build a motor car for the great multitude... constructed of the best materials, by the best men to be hired, after the simplest designs that modern engineering can devise...so low in price that no man making a good salary will be unable to own one-and enjoy with his family the blessing of hours of pleasure in God's great open spaces."

Henry Ford's Vision:

"I will build a motor car for the great multitude... constructed of the best materials, by the best men to be hired, after the simplest designs that modern engineering can devise...so low in price that no man making a good salary will be unable to own one-and enjoy with his family the blessing of hours of pleasure in God's great open spaces."

Recipe for Satisfaction

1 Create a Vision

Tip: We overestimate what they can do in a day, but underestimate what we can do in a year.

Checklist:
- ☐ Imaginable?
- ☐ Desirable?
- ☐ Feasible?
- ☐ Focussed?
- ☐ Flexible (so individuals can act)
- ☐ Communicable?

Further Reading:

John P Kotter - Leading Change (2012)
https://www.amazon.co.uk/Leading-Change-New-Preface-Author/dp/1422186431/

Foundations of Founding

1 ▶ How does my greatest passion fulfil the world's greatest need?

2 ▶ If money was no object, what would I dedicate my time to?

3 ▶ What would I like my grandchildren to tell others I had left behind me?

Says who?!

e.g. I am running a marathon in 2019.

1.

2.

3.

4.

5.

2 Be Accountable

Reference

Joseph Folkman - The '8 Great' Accountability Skills For Business Success
http://www.forbes.com/sites/joefolkman/2014/11/14/how-do-you-score-the-8-great-accountability-skills-for-business-success/#4bf2266d4820

ACCOUNTability

▷ It's as much what we didn't do or avoided doing as what we did do that gets us into rough water. Either way, identifying our own contribution is vital if we are to be positioned to take action.

▷ Being accountable means knowing deep down that everything that happens is either CREATED, PROMOTED, or ALLOWED by you.

▷ My dad once claimed he got a CEO job completely by luck. So I asked him:
"Did you get through an interview?" – YES.
"Did you get an offer?" – YES.
"Did you accept the offer? – YES .
"And you could have said 'no'? – YES.
Bottom line, there were a couple of vital ways in which he had created the job!

2 Be Accountable Worksheet

1 ▶ How did I contribute / what did I actually do?

2 ▶ What would the 'other person' say I did?

Tip: Ask yourself: "How did I create, promote or allow this to happen to me?"

Checklist:

Look out for: *should, could, ought to, must* and *try* in your inbox.

Replace with: *will* or *will not*.

Further Reading:

Who Will Do What By When - Tom Hanson
https://www.amazon.com/Improve-Performance-Accountability-Trust-Integrity/dp/0972419446

e.g. Failed to create a detailed budget.

Spent $30,000 on trade show stand (too much!)

Met with staff every six months (too little!)

2 Thou Shalt Not "Should"

Is that *can't* or *WON'T*?

'What if I create, promote or allow everything that happens to me?'

OLD LANGUAGE

- Should / Should not
- Must / Must not
- Have to
- Can't

NEW LANGUAGE

- Will / will not
- Choose to / Choose not to

3 Take Responsibility

If 'Accountability' explains how I create the present, 'Responsibility' is being 'willing and able to respond'.

mistake

Quote

"The price of greatness is responsibility.

- Winston Churchill

Reference

Statue of Responsibility:
https://en.wikipedia.org/wiki/
Statue_of_Responsibility

▶ Like the word suggests, acting responsibly requires being willing and able to respond. Being willing and not able, or able but not willing is not sufficient.

▶ People are not stupid. We only act for a reason - to avoid pain or gain pleasure. I may need to look a little deeper to understand why I continue apparently undesirable habits.

▶ Emotions are wholly reliable, uncensored, pure responses to situations. Negative feelings are clues that there is something I could be doing but am avoiding.

3 Guidelines for Responsibility

Responsibility is not something you can give someone. It's something that you can choose to take...or not.

☐ Am I able to respond?
☐ Am I willing to respond?

Accountability vs. Responsibility -- What's the Difference?

http://www.investorguide.com/article/15946/accountability-vs-responsibility-d1502/

How to know if you are acting responsibly:

mistake

1. Pay attention to negative emotions
These are the best indicators that you have other courses of action open to you; you're just avoiding them!

2. Never blame others for what you experience.
Because a) their experience is likely not the same as yours and b) all human behaviour has +ve intention behind it, including yours!

3. Never blame yourself
Giving yourself a hard time over unforeseen consequences of decisions you make is irresponsible - makes you feel depressed - a victim. Not a good state in which to make good decisions.

4. Listen to ALL the voices in your head
...including those giving advice you don't like! Often the 'still small voice'.

5. Decide what you want, and take a step
The irresponsible approach is to wait for people or circumstances to change around you. Clue: they a) won't or b) will change in ways you didn't plan for.

6. Recognise the benefits of remaining stuck
Remember you do things for a reason - smoking, drinking, wasting time on Facebook etc. Responsibility requires truly understanding the benefit and finding alternatives that deliver the same benefit.

The irresponsible approach is to keep pretending you'll change.

7. Consider ALL the choices available
Don't go with the first option that comes to mind, that's irresponsible. Generate at least three options before making a decision. You'll be surprised how many more pop up when you get thinking.

Foundations of Founding

4 Keep Commitments

Keeping Commitments is the basic building block of self-belief, and the trust of others.

Reference

10 Lessons For Entrepreneurs on Building Trust
https://www.forbes.com/sites/martinzwilling/2013/07/04/10-lessons-for-entrepreneurs-on-building-trust/#5324ac273a26

▶ Think about those you would trust. How did they earn that trust? Chances are, over time, these are people who have kept their commitments to you.

▶ Keeping promises 100% is the basic building block of self trust, and generates the trust of others as a direct consequence. Armed with a compelling vision and unshakable self trust, anything becomes possible.

▶ The winning margin at the highest level is in the mind. And the winning habit breeds more winning. 'Believe it and then you'll see it' is the how great founders make the world a better place.

4 Clear the Decks Worksheet

Set the bar low to start with. Clearing a low bar often is more motivating than knocking off a high bar.

Set tasks for:

- ☐ Health
- ☐ Work
- ☐ Home
- ☐ Family / Friends
- ☐ Finance
- ☐ Leisure
- ☐ Learning
- ☐ Giving

Visual Teams: Graphic Tools for Commitment, Innovation, and High Performance: http://eu.wiley.com/WileyCDA/WileyTitle/productCd-1118077431.html

1 ▶	**Write list of all outstanding tasks** (a one time exercise)
2 ▶	**Delete those you wish to relieve yourself of.**
3 ▶	**Put names next to those you will now delegate.**
4 ▶	**Allocate 'do or die' deadlines to the remaining tasks.**

Outstanding tasks	Name	Deadline
Complete Tax Return	Me	1 April

4 Keep Commitments 100%

Kept commitments generate:	Broken commitments generate:
• The trust of others • Improved relationships • Greater self-trust & self-confidence • More awareness & participation	• Loss of trust of others • Deteriorating relationships • Loss of self-trust & self-confidence • Confusion, tiredness & withdrawal

Make commitments important by:

• Writing them down (including time).
• Only making agreements you intend to keep.
• Being willing to say 'no'.
• Renegotiating with integrity if circumstances change.

5 Get Organised

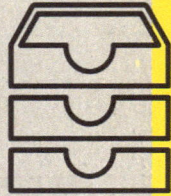

Time spent planning saves untold hours in execution.

Quote

"Organizing is what you do before you do something, so that when you do it, it is not all mixed up."
- A.A. Milne

Reference

What Everyone Needs to Know to Be More Productive

https://hbr.org/2015/04/what-everyone-needs-to-know-to-be-more-productive

▶ Things don't happen generally, they happen specifically, and usually in small, incremental steps.

▶ Having a written and visible plan is a great way for others to know how they can help.

▶ Sadly we do the urgent non-important tasks first (the bosses' priorities!), urgent important next (daily crises), non-urgent non-important (check email, eat lunch) and lastly non-urgent important - things that will make a long term impact.

WHAT DOESN'T WORK:

	URGENT	Not urgent
IMPORTANT	1	4
Not important	2	3

WHAT WORKS:

	URGENT	Not urgent
IMPORTANT	2	1
Not important	3	4

5 Get Organised Worksheet

Checklist:

- [ ] List bite size tasks.
- [ ] Add deadline.
- [ ] Delegate where possible.
- [ ] Highlight when done, DON'T just 'cross out' or 'delete'.

Further Reading:

Harvard Business Review Productivity:
https://hbr.org/topic/productivity

1 ▶ Which aspect of work or life would benefit most from being organised right now?

2 ▶ If you had 30 minutes today, what could you re-organise to great effect?

3 ▶ How do you share your plans with others?

e.g. 50th Party for Bob (Oct 14)

5 Get Organised

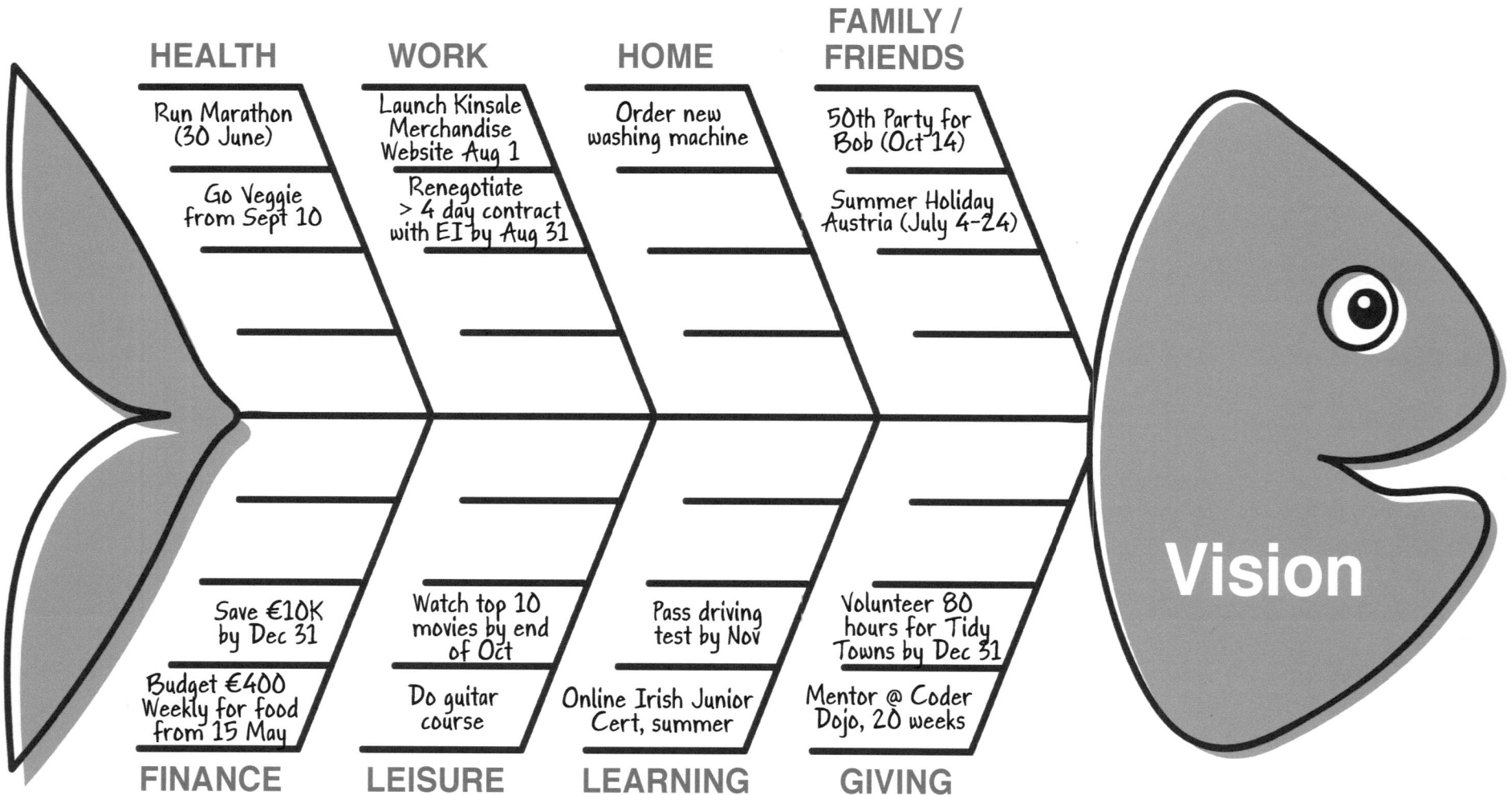

HEALTH
- Run Marathon (30 June)
- Go Veggie from Sept 10

WORK
- Launch Kinsale Merchandise Website Aug 1
- Renegotiate > 4 day contract with EI by Aug 31

HOME
- Order new washing machine

FAMILY / FRIENDS
- 50th Party for Bob (Oct 14)
- Summer Holiday Austria (July 4-24)

Vision

FINANCE
- Save €10K by Dec 31
- Budget €400 Weekly for food from 15 May

LEISURE
- Watch top 10 movies by end of Oct
- Do guitar course

LEARNING
- Pass driving test by Nov
- Online Irish Junior Cert, summer

GIVING
- Volunteer 80 hours for Tidy Towns by Dec 31
- Mentor @ Coder Dojo, 20 weeks

6 Keep Score

MAY

What gets measured, gets done.

Reference

The AARRR Startup Metrics model developed by Dave McClure.
http://startitup.co/guides/374/aarrr-startup-metrics

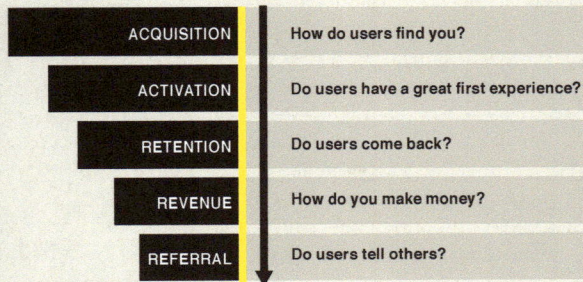

ACQUISITION	How do users find you?
ACTIVATION	Do users have a great first experience?
RETENTION	Do users come back?
REVENUE	How do you make money?
REFERRAL	Do users tell others?

Foundations of Founding

▶ Most measures of success - sales/profits/number of customers - tell us where we've been, and not where we're going (Lag indicators). We need measures of the future (Lead indicators) such as % of sales from new products, net promoter score.

▶ Performance reviews for individuals or teams are the clearest example of the importance of keeping score. Only the concrete goals/KPIs get discussed, and go on to inform pay rises and other rewards.

▶ Keeping score also provides motivation, specially if the metrics are clear, and easily understood. Today we can measure an athletes' performance in incredible detail, in real time. By just knowing you completed 100m in 10.2 seconds sums it all up nicely! British Airways once boiled its entire operational scorecard down to a single metric - number of flights leaving on time - having worked out that all other activities were contributory factors. Most businesses don't look beyond the obvious financial indicators to help them understand where they're headed.

15

6 Keep Score Worksheet

Tip: Remember even governments have measures for abstract metrics like "consumer confidence", on which rest entire national economic strategies.

Checklist:

☐ **Does this help our people?**
☐ **Does this help our customers?**
(courtesy Warren Buffett)

Further Reading:

Balanced Scorecard: https://www.amazon.com/Balanced-Scorecard-Translating-Strategy-Action/dp/0875846513/ref=tmm_hrd_swatch_0?_encoding=UTF8&qid=1500546607&sr=8-1

1 ▶ **Do we only have metrics for the past? (sales/profits) Do we have measures indicating a future? (% of repeat customers)**

2 ▶ **Do we have ways to measure how we uphold our values?**

3 ▶ **Do we have independent validation of our metrics?**

e.g. Sales Revenue

6 A Balanced Scoreboard

e.g. Total number of customers

Lag Indicators → Lead Indicators

e.g. Percentage of new customers

Fiscal Management

Creative Opportunities

e.g. Customer Retention

e.g. Customer satisfaction

Process Improvements

Quality & Service Opportunities

7 Acknowledge Effort

Appreciation of effort is 10x more motivating than judgement of results.

A bad harvest doesn't make a bad farmer.

Reference

The Powerful Impact of Acknowledging Good Work by Laura Garnet

https://www.inc.com/laura-garnett/acknowledgment-the-new-charisma-at-work.html

▶ Everything starts with an idea in the head of an individual. Getting started (doing just anything) is the next step. Completing the task successfully, even after many failed attempts is NOT the end. "Acknowledgement' - of self or others - is what generates commitment, creativity, collaboration to go on.

▶ Distinguish between 'judging results' and 'acknowledging effort'. No benefit from judging results, but huge payoff for applauding genuine effort. Self acknowledgement is even more important than appreciation of others, because I'm the only one who really knows if I gave it my best shot.

▶ No such thing as right/wrong decisions - just choices and consequences. Feeling wrong just damages my confidence.

7 Acknowledge Effort Worksheet

1 ▶ **How do you feel when you thank someone for their contribution?**

2 ▶ **What's it like to give a gift v. receiving one?**

Tip: Just say a genuine "thank you" when you notice someone making an effort. Try looking into their eyes as you say it.

Checklist:

Make a note of 3 things to be grateful for each day.

☐ _____

☐ _____

☐ _____

Further Reading:

The Benefits of Cultivating an Attitude of Gratitude: https://www.psychologytoday.com/blog/some-assembly-required/201411/the-benefits-cultivating-attitude-gratitude

Examples
Send thank you email

Names
Gwen

7 Cycle of Completion

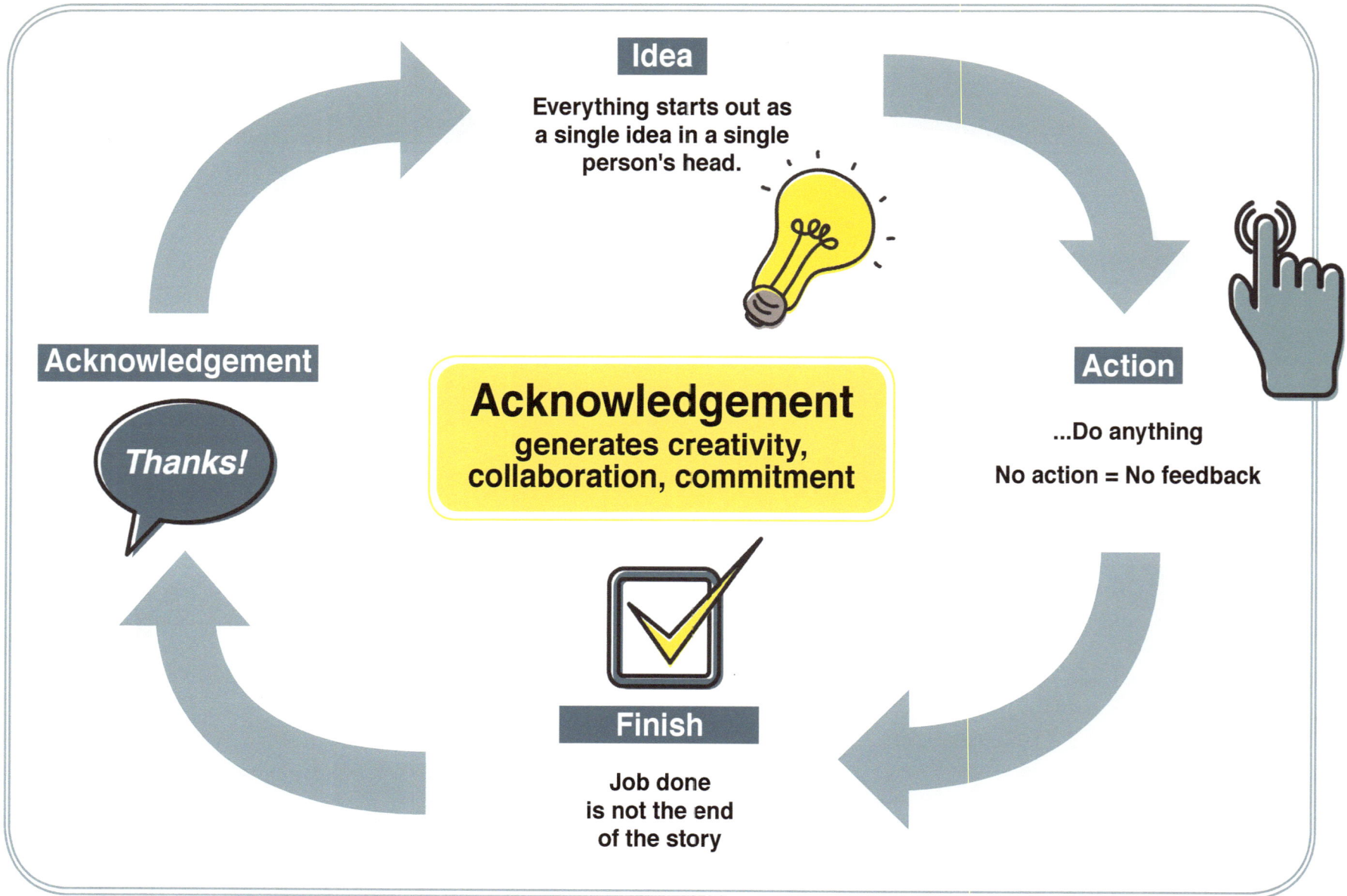

Idea

Everything starts out as a single idea in a single person's head.

Action

...Do anything

No action = No feedback

Finish

Job done is not the end of the story

Acknowledgement

Thanks!

Acknowledgement generates creativity, collaboration, commitment

8 Master Relationships

Tried doing everything on your own? That's why great relationships are critical.

Quote

> If we could read the secret history of our enemies, we should find in each man's life sorrow and suffering enough to disarm all hostility.
> — Henry Wadsworth Longfellow

Reference

Influencing with Integrity by Genie Z. Laborde

https://books.google.ie/books?id=VNG17Gme_REC&printsec=frontcover#v=onepage&q&f=false

▶ There are two aspects to working with other people - the task and the relationship. While there is a good relationship there is always the chance to deliver on the task. But when the relationship breaks down, the task becomes impossible.

▶ Don't concern yourself with trying to change others. The only person you will ever be in control of is - YOU! If you change your behaviour, you will get a changed response, because relationships are like systems. Changed input = changed output.

▶ People do not buy from people they don't like. And for that reason alone we need to master our relationships to stand any chance of success. Neither was there ever a self-made man or woman. Steve Jobs had his Steve Wozniak, Bill Gates had his Paul Allen, Batman had Robin; and Thelma, Louise.

8 Master Relationships Worksheet

1 ▶ Who else would it be good to strike up a relationship with?

2 ▶ What would they really appreciate from me?

It's yellow!

It's blue!

Checklist:

Who are your 12 most important relationships? What score (1-10) would you give each relationship for:
a) being effective/getting results and
b) being warm v. cold!

Tip: Ask what those people would really appreciate from you, that would improve the relationship.

Further Reading:

Johari Window technique to help better understand your relationship with themselves and others:
http://kevan.org/johari

	Name:	Relationship Score (1-10)	Effectiveness Score (1-10)	What would they like?
e.g.	Paul	9	9	Organise gym membership
1				
2				
3				
4				
5				
6				
7				
8				
9				
10				
11				
12				

Foundations of Founding

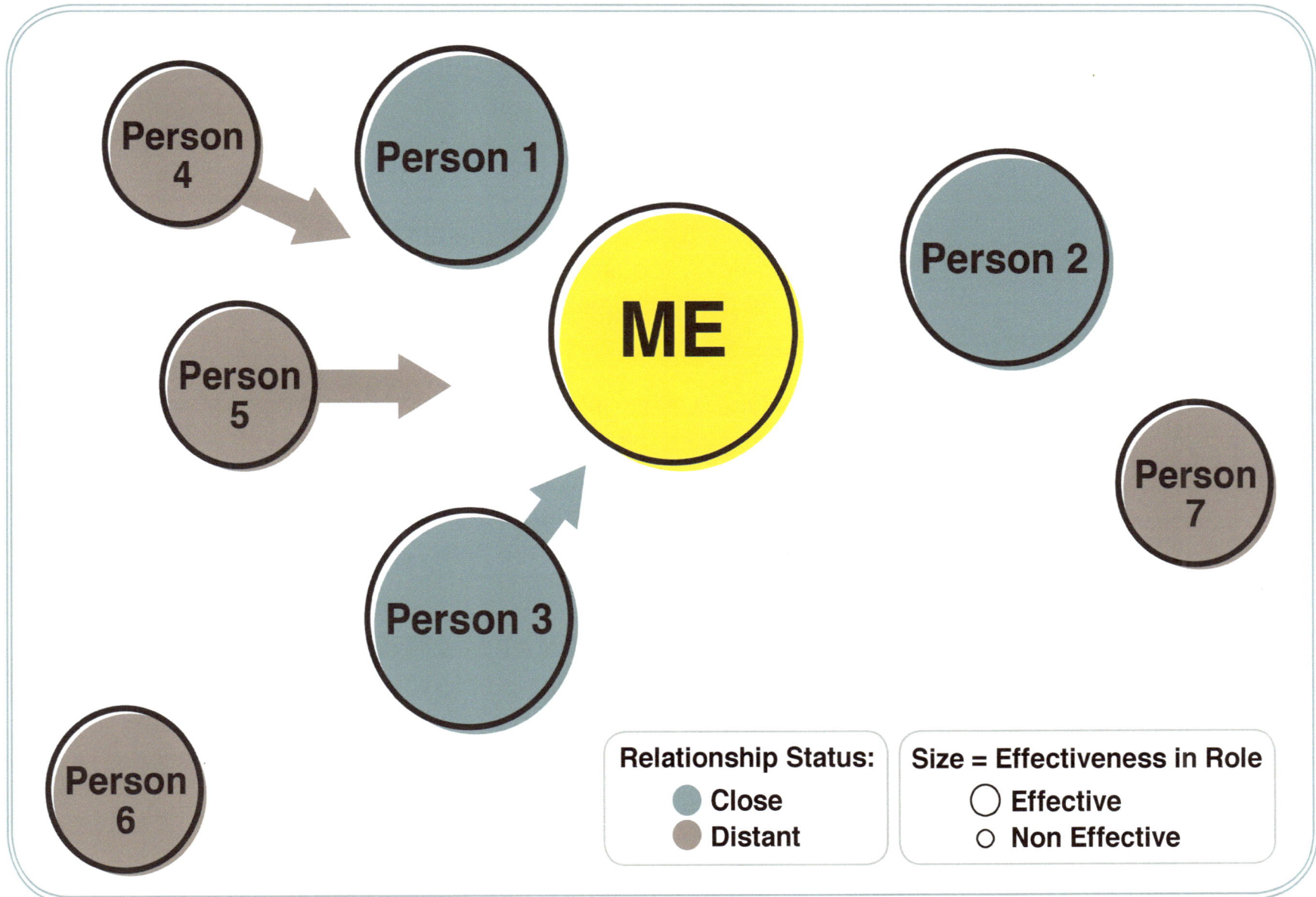

8 Evaluate Key Relationships

Person 4

Person 1

ME

Person 2

Person 5

Person 3

Person 7

Person 6

Relationship Status:
● Close
● Distant

Size = Effectiveness in Role
○ Effective
○ Non Effective

9 Try Everything

Quote

"It always seems impossible until it's done."
- Nelson Mandela

Reference

14 Famous Business Pivots by Jason Nazar

https://www.forbes.com/sites/jasonnazar/2013/10/08/14-famous-business-pivots/#1c80a5f35797

▶ Having two options is the definition of a dilemma. Choice requires at least three options; when you get to that point the fourth and fifth flow more easily.

▶ One way to get at least three different options is to ask yourself what you'd do if:
a) Your life depended on it?
b) Your best friend/partner's life depended on it?
c) Your child's life depended on it?

▶ Set up an imaginary board of directors or role models. Read stories about people you admire, get to know not only what they did, but what was important to them. Their values. And imagine yourself applying those values to your current circumstances.

THINK
VISUAL

Orla Kelly
Publishing

Foundations
of Founding

www.ingramcontent.com/pod-product-compliance
Lightning Source LLC
Chambersburg PA
CBHW041259210326

41598CB00009B/847